D1230781

JOB SEARCH
For Moms

Nancy Range Anderson

JOB SEARCH for Moms
By Nancy Range Anderson

The publisher, producer, and author shall not be liable for any loss or damages relative to the content in this book. Application of the material is at the discretion of the user.

No part of this publication may be reproduced, stored in a retrieval system, or transmitted in any form other than as may be permitted by the publisher.

Copyright © 2010 by Lulu.com. All rights reserved.

ISBN 978-0-557-31707-3

ABOUT THE AUTHOR

Nancy Range Anderson is the President of Blackbird Learning Associates, LLC a company that specializes in job search training. Nancy is a solution-driven training & development leader with over 25 years experience in Human Resources and Learning & Development in the pharmaceutical, finance and insurance industries. Known for her excellent facilitation skills, Nancy teaches resume preparation, interviewing, networking, and career change tactics to individuals and groups. Nancy is a Board Member of Family and Community Services of Somerset County NJ and a member of the Middlesex Area Women's Club. She lives in New Jersey with her husband Matthew and children Caitlin and Christian. Nancy enjoys offering career guidance to displaced workers.

CONTENTS

4

INTRODUCTION

The purpose of this book is to help you become better able to manage the job searching venture. Even though you may have had several such ventures, this book is sure to provide you with some good tips and ideas that can help you improve your rate of success. Throughout this book you'll find lots of examples and tools you can use to create your own schedules, ways to track your progress, and ideas for corresponding with the people who can help you find your next employment.

In the first chapter, "Assessing," focusing on you, your skills, and the careers that are right for you is always the first step in any job searching venture. In the second chapter, "Networking," building relationships, gaining knowledge, and finding employment is highlighted. In the third chapter, "Presenting," how to build a resume, write cover letters, and participate in interviews is addressed.

◊ ◊ ◊

1

ASSESSING

Self-assessing is one of the first steps in any job searching venture. When conducting an assessment of your readiness for job searching, the focus should be on you, the skills you possess, and the careers that may be right for you.

Focus on You

Focusing on you will help you to make personal discoveries about your current status. When you focus on you consider how reflecting, planning, and updating each plays a role in your preparedness for job searching.

Reflecting

When we conduct a self-assessment we generally reflect upon who we are as a person and what our status is at the present time. Reflecting typically requires us to review our emotional, financial, and external issues.

On an emotional level, consider your current state of mind. Depending on your situation and the reasons behind your job search, your emotions may vary. Acting upon your emotions can become an important first step in understanding your unique skill set and abilities. If you were displaced or outsourced in your current job you may experience tumultuous emotions like confusion, anger, loss of confidence, or worry. You might even feel a sense of exhilaration. Your feelings are normal and an essential part of your growth. Whether you enjoyed it, your job played a role in defining you as an individual. It also validated you as a contributor and member of a social group. Much like a death or divorce, once your job is eliminated, grieving is common. Similarly, it is important to take care of yourself while preparing to move ahead. Accept your emotions and be mindful of your needs like diet, exercise, and the proper amount of sleep. If you have decided to leave your company voluntarily, you should consider your reasons for leaving and the decisions or events that caused you leave. This is a wonderful opportunity for self discovery and reflection. Another set of emotions universal to most mothers comes with the decision to return to work after a break. Studies indicate that although working is a financial necessity, many of us return to work for confirmation as a contributor, a role model, or a desire for more. Sorting through emotions is a gradual process and it helps to have support, guidance, and a plan. "Emotional Management" lists steps that may assist with emotional reflecting.

Emotional Management

1. Accept and validate your feelings.
2. Journal your feelings.
3. List the events, achievements, and decisions made in your previous employment.
4. Inventory your concerns about beginning the job search.
5. Socialize and it translates into networking.

We need to consider our financial status when we reflect upon our circumstances. The duration for a job search lasts about seven months, so it becomes necessary to monitor your finances monthly. Consider the state of the economy, the availability of jobs in your industry, available income from other family members, company severance packages, unemployment benefits, and your savings. Consider the cost of any training or education needs. Create a means to plan and track your expenses. "Monthly Expenditures" is a device that helps you track and reflect on your financial status for a few months at a time. This model spans a four-month period. You can construct yours however you like. Insert the expenses to track in your own circumstances. Begin with your income for each month and finish by totaling your expenses.

Monthly Expenditures

	January	February	March	April
Monthly Income:				
Monthly Expenses:				
Housing				
Utilities				
Food				
Healthcare				
School				
Vehicle				
Clothing				
Dues/Subscriptions				
Entertainment				
Misc.				
Total Expenses				

As you reflect on your financial condition, think about those expenses that you can eliminate or postpone. When faced with financial uncertainty, contact creditors to inform them of your employment status. They will often help you in developing a payment plan.

Reflecting is also a time to assess any external constraints that might prevent you from finding a job. External constraints are those real or perceived issues that may present roadblocks that are potentially beyond your control or that you need to overcome. Develop your own "External Constraints Checklist" that captures a number of common roadblocks.

External Constraints Checklist

1. Support: Once you have made the decision to begin the job search, it is a good idea to gather your support "team" consisting of family and friends.
2. Economic Times: The state of the economy and its impact on you and your family is a major consideration when focusing on career change and it needs to be thoroughly examined and discussed. Should your career focus include additional training, consider grants, free training, or other options before finalizing any decisions.
3. Transportation Needs: We need to be at work on time and as scheduled, so it is imperative that we include transportation needs in our thought process.
4. Child Care: We must consider daycare and after-school programs.
5. Health Issues: The Family Medical Leave Act and Americans with Disabilities Act prohibits discrimination based upon health issues, pregnancy, or disability.

Planning

Planning plays a significant role in our assessment process. All effective planning requires preparing, goal setting, and doing research.

Planning is envisioning an end goal and then mapping a course to get there. When beginning a job search we tend to prepare by thinking about updating our resumes and sharpening our interviewing skills, but this actually comes a bit later. There are a number of steps involved in preparation and they can be divided into two categories. The first is creating a list of your career likes, dislikes and aspirations. Think about the statements in "Career Assessment" and answer them as thoroughly as you can.

Career Assessment

1. What did I like about my last job?
2. What activities did I enjoy in my last job?
3. What types of work energizes me?
4. What about my last job did I dislike?
5. What types of tasks do I dislike?
6. If could do anything, what would it be?
7. What tasks are involved in my dream job?

The second phase in preparation involves setting the stage for your job search. Organizing your work space and having the proper tools to start and maintain your plan are a necessity. Your space should be clutter free and without distraction. Any room or location in your home will work or you may want to go to the library or another location. If you have a computer, Internet access is key since your preparation will involve research. If computer access not available in your home, the library is again a good alternative. You will need to professionally update your e-mail address and voice mail message. Other tools to have on hand are paper, pens, calculator and a calendar.

Goal setting is a fundamental part of any business planning process. Here too, it should it be a vital part of our job search plan. Setting goals allows us to visualize our future, clarify our steps, and focus on dates. It is the cornerstone of the job search planning process in that it allows us to focus on necessary steps while weeding out any needless distractions. It is also highly motivating and a useful way to measure our time and progress. Within the context of the job search, our goals should be written in specific terms, they should have precise time frames, and they should be measurable. A specific goal tells us exactly what we want to accomplish. It is helpful to break each broad goal statement into manageable smaller statements. This step not only keeps us on track, but it allows us to feel a sense of accomplishment when each step is achieved. A time oriented goal statement should include specific target dates and the approximate time we will need to complete each of the steps. A measurable goal statement should include concrete criteria or action steps that will allow us to measure our progress. Setting goals in the planning process allows us to focus and move in the right direction. It also gives us a sense of purpose or accomplishment to check off each action item as we move forward. Try using the "Resume Development Checklist" to create your goal statement and take the necessary steps toward producing the resume.

Resume Development Checklist

Prepare final version of resume by August 12, 20__.

---

1. Identify areas of expertise.
2. Choose resume template.
3. Create career history.
4. Create summary statement.
5. Type first draft using selected template.
6. Get feedback from contacts.
7. Type final version.

Research is gathering the facts and data to prepare for moving forward in the job search. Now that we have established our career likes and dislikes and mapped out the steps we need to follow in goal setting, now isolate the careers that interest us. Career information, including the skills needed for various jobs, regional salaries, and future trends can be found from many sources. Internet searches yield quite a bit of information. Governmental sites, including the Bureau of Labor Statistics provides detailed descriptions of hundreds of jobs nationally. The site also includes any skills needed, working conditions, job trends, and earnings. By searching a particular job it is possible to narrow your focus by identifying certain skill sets. Online newspapers and magazines usually provide daily recaps of the state of the economy, forecasted employment needs, and hints for the job seeker. Many career types have associated professional groups and often these groups list the skills needed by its members. Many of these groups host local chapter meetings where you can visit and gain additional information by talking with the members. Your local libraries are an informative source on job search tactics. The librarian can direct you to the latest resources in career development. Colleges or trade schools are another resource. A career counselor at your local university or community college may provide information on employment trends and the education or training needed for development. Visit the employment office serving your area. These offices offer a variety of assistance with your job search. Another valuable research option is to meet with an individual whose profession appeals to you. This type of research can further clarify your interest in and alignment to a particular job.

Updating

Once you have identified your career aspirations and established your goals, review your skills to determine if they need to be updated. Consider your developmental needs in education, training, and mentoring.

Our education can determine the career path we chose. Some jobs require a high school education. Others specify college, while others require advanced degrees. If a job specifies a specific level of education, we need to ask ourselves if we are educationally prepared to pursue that particular position. Lately, many organizations use electronic scanners to sift through the resumes they receive. The skills and education for a job are entered into the scanner and the resumes are "read" to determine if a candidate matches the job requirements. If we do not have the education required for a job, our resume will be discarded. Network with someone with a similar job and ask about the education necessary for the position. Many times you can get a better perspective on the position by speaking directly with someone who is currently holding the job. Contact a local university or community college for direction on your educational needs. If you decide you need some education, look for institutions that will assign credits for work experience. Adults have experience that can be converted into college credit. A career counselor can assist you in determining any educational needs for the current job market.

Training comes in many forms, depending on your specific administrative, management, or technical needs. "Training Needs Assessment" provides a list of questions to help guide your decision making.

Training Needs Assessment

1. What new skills do I need to learn?
2. What existing skills need to be refreshed?
3. Where do I need additional knowledge?
4. What can I do to build upon my strengths or weaknesses?
5. Who in my support group or network can help me?
6. What reading material can I use?
7. What course should I take?

Once you have established your training needs, there are various free or low cost methods that you can use to update them. "Training Resources" provides a list of the possibilities.

Training Resources

1. Library: Most libraries offer free sessions on using the Internet, designing a Web site or everyday software packages such as word processing, spreadsheets, and chart creation.
2. Community College: Semester catalogs.
3. Colleges or Universities: "Senior" discounts.
4. Adult School: Most towns offer evening classes on a number of business classes.
5. Bartering: Trade talents with a friend who has a skill set that you'd like to learn.
6. Online Courses: Available in a variety of

---

topics and many are free.
7. Unemployment Office: Software training.
8. Computer: Tutorials in using software.
9. Network: Friends, neighbors, family, and co-workers offer training resources.
10. Temp Agencies: Computer training.
11. Current Employer: Employee seminars and career development.

At some point in our business or in our personal lives we may have had someone who provided guidance or support, was willing to listen, and offered valuable feedback. These individuals offer mentoring. Mentoring is the ability of one person, the mentor, to impart lessons learned or information to another person, the mentee. "Learn all you can from the mistakes of others. You won't have time to make them all yourself" (Alfred Sheinwold). Look for life coaches who can impart their knowledge in a more strategic fashion. These lessons can include an understanding of organizational culture, and the skills needed to navigate through professional, technical, and business related ventures. A mentor can enhance your understanding of your professional skills and abilities and provide career guidance, feedback, and encouragement. If you decide to work with a mentor, it is important to make a serious effort to continually maintain and sustain the integrity of the relationship. Observe the points in "Mentor Selection Matrix."

Mentor Selection Matrix

Mentor Role:

1. Provides constructive evaluation.

2. Communicates well.
3. Invests time.
4. Challenges you to create and maintain your career path.
5. Desires to see you succeed.

Mentee Role:

1. Asks for and is receptive to feedback.
2. Addresses feedback.
3. Seeks to be challenged.
4. Takes action on suggestions.
5. Asks questions and listens.
6. Observes how the mentor communicates, addresses tasks, solves problems, and relates to organizational situations.
7. Invests time.
8. Shares job search goals.
9. Takes responsibility for the job search.

Mutual Roles:

1. Agrees on mentoring schedule.
2. Communicates honestly.
3. Works confidentially.
4. Discusses shared experiences.
5. Explores current and alternative job search experiences.

Focus on Skills

The job search process involves planning and focus. When we focus on our skills, we are examining our skills that are personal, professional, and transferable. In this section, we will further explore our core work values,

17

interests, and personality. We will also look at our unique skill sets and the skills that we currently use that can be transferred to other jobs or careers.

Personal

Before you can identify the career direction you want to assume you need to evaluate your work values, interests, and personality. These will help you determine the type of career that will be the most meaningful and provide added value to your life.

You have already identified the type of work and activities that you enjoy and that give you satisfaction. To help you further identify your career aspirations, you will now inventory your work values. This step is part of a career decision making strategy that will allow you to focus on the types of jobs that motivate you. Your work values are a part of your core being and are influenced by your background, belief system, and the way you were brought up. There are a number of free or low cost work value inventories available on the Internet. The values covered are varied, but generally fall into two categories: 1) the work environment and 2) the job requirements. Use the "Personal Work Values" chart to rank the various categories and their importance to you.

Personal Work Values

Work Value	Rank as High, Medium or Low Importance
The Work Environment:	
Salary and Benefits	
Retirement or Savings Plan	

Job Security
Working Conditions
Work/Family Friendly
Telecommuting Options
Diversity

Job Requirements:

Status or Position
Autonomy
Managing Others
Challenging
Creativity
Recognition
Power
Teamwork
Influence Others

By identifying your core work values, you are better prepared to research the industries and businesses that are suited to you. Is research, problem solving, or project planning of interest to you? Are writing, creating, or designing motivating? Would you rather help people or are you more mechanically inclined? For years, students from middle school through college have taken career interest inventories that help answer these questions.

The same principles apply to identifying career interests. Matching them with a variety of occupations are the foundations for all career interest inventories for any age. As a critical planning tool, the career interest inventory allows us to determine our work-related likes and dislikes. Once on the job our career interests help validate our job satisfaction, that inner contentment and pride we have with our job.

The Internet offers many free or low cost career interest inventory tools. You may choose to use these or solicit the expertise and advice of a career counselor. Career interest inventories will ask you many questions, all relating to your likes and dislikes pertaining to a variety of workplace activities. The questions are varied, numerous, and relate to whether your career interests are more creative, enterprising, investigative, conventional, or social. Once your career interests are indentified, many sites will automatically flesh out career options. You can further refine this information by comparing the data from the inventory survey to the skill sets listed in the hundreds of positions offered on occupational Web sites. The Occupational Outlook Handbook and O*NET are good governmental resources. In addition to analyzing these, review your network, support contacts, or work with your mentor to devise a plan to further define your interests and matching occupations. You should narrow down your list of career interests to under ten occupations. "Investigative Suggestions" lists behaviors to help you narrow your interests.

Investigative Suggestions

1. Volunteer at a non-profit organization.
2. Lead an activity or use your technical skills in your community.
3. Read and research open job positions to analyze the descriptions and your career interests.
4. Participate in informational interviews.

You may remember working at a profession that didn't suit you. It could have been caused by a number of factors including the work itself, the clients, the manager or your co-workers. In many cases, that discontent had to do with your personality type. Personality type or style inventories measure our behavior in certain situations and provide specific feedback on our likes, dislikes, attitudes, motivators, and work styles. A personality inventory is a good indicator of the type of occupations that are suitable for you. Our personalities are made up of a number of intrinsic values that we were either born with or learned as we grew up. These factors are the foundation of our personalities and they should be seriously considered when preparing for a career change or job. Try using some personality type indicators like MBTI or Myers Briggs Assessment. These kinds of assessments, based upon the studies of C.G. Jung on psychological types, measures personality types and provides input on how we perceive the world and make decisions. The information gathered from this tool is generally a good indicator of your motivators and needs in a particular job. There are a number of other very helpful tools and these can be researched on the Internet or in your library. The Keirsey Temperament Sorter is used to identify career focus, improve relationships, and reduce conflict. The DiSC Behavioral Assessment is an easy to administer survey designed to identify our personal styles, motivating factors, and preferred work environment. It is based upon the research of William Moulton Marston to ascertain the careers suitable for your personality.

Professional

As you have seen, there are a number of personal factors to consider when planning a job search or career change. Another area to reflect upon is your professional skill set; the expertise you have gathered through your experiences, competencies, and aspirations.

Over the years we develop specific abilities from previous jobs. Internet or paper-based tools help us to categorize our experiences into skills. Inventory your own skills by creating a list of the jobs and experiences that you have had over the past 10-15 years. Sort them into categories like management, professional, and administrative support. Management skills are those that you may have used or gained while supervising a staff or department. Office or administrative skills are support skills. Professional skills cover any number of abilities from your trade or career. They are varied and cover areas such as technical skills, research, development, scientific, financial, teaching, and many others. Capture your work experience as well as any volunteer or outside activities. While plotting your skills and abilities, you may notice that they may transfer into a variety of categories. Appraise your strengths and assess your weaknesses. Create a matrix like "Strengths and Weaknesses Appraisal" to perform your assessment.

Strengths and Weakness Appraisal		
Activity	Company	S/W
Management Skills		
Creating Objectives		S
Coaching Performance		S
Conducting Appraisals		S
Budgeting		W
Professional Skills		
Vendor Negotiation		W
Client Communication		S
Writing		S
Communications		S

Develop Training	S
Facilitate	S
Administrative Skills	
Reporting	W

Competencies can be defined as the clusters or groups of behaviors that enable us to behave in an excellent manner. Often called "soft" skills, they are the skills that can enhance or distract a business activity. Competencies can be grouped into many different categories and many companies use them in their hiring practices. You will often see job ads requiring you are a team player, able to negotiate with clients, or having good communication skills. For your job search it is vital to identify your "core competencies," and categorize them as either strengths or limitations. To accomplish this, we need to examine our past positions and activities and identify the competencies that supported our work activities. The following chart lists five of the more common competencies used in a work environment. Review each definition and evaluate it using the "Core Competencies Assessment." This model helps you to check your strengths and limitations in some of the most sought-after skills and competencies.

Core Competencies Assessment	
Competency	Strength or Limitation
Communication:	
The ability to express, transmit and interpret of knowledge and ideas. Includes speaking, writing, teaching,	

training, interpreting.

Planning:

Forming an account of the steps
needed to achieve a goal within a
certain time frame. Includes setting
goals and tasks, project management,
follow-through, time management.

Analytical/Problem Solving:

The ability to visualize, state, and solve
complex problems and situations and
make decisions. Includes proactive
problem solving steps, critical thinking
and idea generation.

Leadership:

 The ability to direct and guide
individuals or groups. This may
include delegation, managing and
evaluate performance, setting goals,
coach, decision making, strategic
thinking, motivation.

Interpersonal Skills:

The ability to relate to others. This
includes vendor, client, peer
interaction, negotiation, teamwork,
valuing diversity, influencing.

You may ask your former manager, peers, mentor, or members of your personal network to provide you with feedback. While completing this assessment, you may notice a commonality between your career interests, values, skills, and competencies.

Never underestimate the value of your dreams and aspirations when starting a job search or considering a career change. Unfortunately, many of us question our own abilities and skills or we discount our dreams due to our daily responsibilities or negative thoughts. We often listen to the opinions of others and this too keeps us from following a path that we had once envisioned. In order to realistically look at your interests, visualize a star like the one in "Staring Your Aspirations."

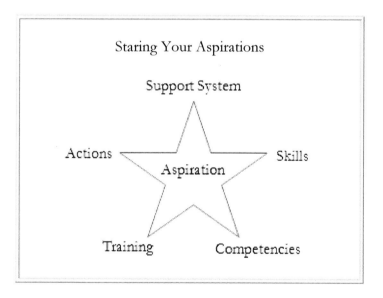

In the center of the star, state your aspiration or dream. The top point of the star is your support system; those people, places, and ideas that can help and sustain you. List the names of those people from organizations who can offer assistance through child or family care, guidance, or other support. The remaining four points of the star are the skills, competencies, training, and actions needed to make your dream a reality. You can establish these pieces by reviewing the previous planning activities you completed while focusing on your personal and professional skills. You will also need to research the training options and action steps needed to explore your career aspirations. Much of this data can be found by visiting your library or local college, speaking with your mentor or a career counselor, or using the Internet.

Transferable

Many of us never consider gaining skills and knowledge from anywhere other than the workplace. Over the years, we have developed hundreds of skills and competencies from sources other than our paid or unpaid employment. We should also consider our volunteering efforts and the work we have done with various outside organizations including schools, clubs, drives, religious affiliations, and sporting teams. Tasks that we perform socially, technically, or organizationally can be grouped into a category called "Transferable Skills." Unlike job-specific skills, transferable skills are universal and can be used across a wide-range of occupations, regardless of position. They are the life skills that transfer to a job.

On a personal or social level, we lead, manage, deliver, arrange, propose, and manage activities or events with our friends, neighbors, peers, and group members. As a volunteer or member of an outside organization we utilize transferable job skills continually. When planning for your job search, consider all of your outside activities. It is helpful to list the task and record all of the activities associated with it. These activities can then be categorized into competencies and included on your resume. As an example, perhaps you are the Chairperson of a fashion show fund raiser for your child's school. There are numerous responsibilities associated with this event and many other parents are involved in the production. Some of the tasks involved in this example include gathering volunteers, planning the function, advertising the event, assigning committee work, and pricing the venue. All of these activities contain valuable transferable job skills like communicating, event planning, negotiating, organizing, delegating, recruiting, project management, fund-raising, coordinating, and leadership.

Technical transferable job skills are similar to personal skills. These are skills that you may use at your current job or outside activities that can again be transferred to a number of other positions. Using office support software packages is an example of technical transferable job skills. Most companies use standardized software for word processing and spreadsheets. Learning these basic applications will go a long way toward helping you find a job in today's high tech environment. Even if you are not currently working, there are other areas where you may be using technical expertise. At home you may already be using technical office products like accounting or budgeting systems and spreadsheets. "Transferable Technical Skills" provides examples of the many useful skills you may also be using with your outside activities.

Transferable Technical Skills

1. Collecting and analyzing data
2. Comparing data
3. Compiling statistics
4. Installing software
5. Interpreting data
6. Recording information
7. Instructing members
8. Troubleshooting
9. Tracking entries/data

---

10. Processing information

Transferable organizational skills are those that we use in our jobs that can be applied to another similar position or to a totally different job. We each have some sort of organizational transferable job skills, but we seldom consider them. Instead, we tend to focus on our occupational skills. Evaluate your transferable skills that are organizational in nature. "Competencies Assessment" lists the many types of competencies you may need to help you make your assessment.

Competencies Assessment

1. Problem solving
2. Budgeting
3. Designing
4. Delivering
5. Managing/Supervising
6. Leading
7. Writing
8. Decision making
9. Estimating
10. Delegation
11. Synthesizing data
12. Support
13. Meeting management
14. Researching
15. Persuading/Negotiating
16. Communicating

With additional training, you might consider making a career change because you have many of the transferable skills required by an employer. Try recording your personal, technical, and organizational transferable skills by listing your current and former jobs, outside service, and other activities in the "Competencies Assessment Worksheet."

Competencies Assessment Worksheet

Job or Activity:	Transferable Skills:
Sales in a bookstore	People and math skills
Secretarial	Computer and organizational skills
Team Leader	Facilitating skills

Complete this list with all of the jobs you might like to pursue and add your transferable skills that apply. Sometimes working this backward is helpful. Begin by listing all of your transferrable skills and match those to jobs for which you are qualified. More than one job can be listed for each set of competencies. Remember, you are a multi-faceted woman who likely has many skills that have been developed over your lifetime. Capture them.

Focus on Careers

When assessing our career options, it is helpful to focus on career clusters. Within these career clusters there are a variety of positions that may or may not be of interest to you. Your research, specifically that which is focused on industry trends and the predictions for future careers should help you narrow your objectives. Recent governmental statistics can be found in the Occupational Handbook from the Bureau of Labor Statistics, which are updated every two years. This is a good place to start your research. Other resources found in your local library or at career centers are also helpful in assessing leadership, scientific, and administrative careers.

Leadership

The role of a leader is vast. There are many skills required of a true leader. Some are natural and others are learned. These skills include communication, trust, vision, influence, integrity, assertiveness and creativity. All are part of training, motivating, and leading a team.

Training requires understanding human behavior and we each can at times behave differently. As a leader, you will need to accept the differences of your staff while ensuring that they are capable of performing their jobs effectively. Training takes effective communication skills, performance management, and developmental planning. In addition to working with a staff, you will need to understand the direction of the business and translate these initiatives into tasks or projects. This too involves training and development activities. In your personal career planning activities, you may have found that your skill set draws upon your preference for leading and that it includes a desire for and a knack for training. In the course of your professional or volunteer activities you may have been asked to train a system, process, or job skill to a group or individual. If these activities are enjoyable to you, count them among your transferable or job skills and look for ways to further apply them through more learning opportunities or training situations.

A leader is generally a motivator. Motivation is a means to empower others to be continually committed to the job and to achieve a desired task. Recent studies show that most employees prefer attention, development, and praising opportunities over the usual corporate financial incentives. There are many skills included under the motivation umbrella including listening, questioning, guiding, fostering relationships, correcting performance, supporting and trusting. If the results of your career assessment indicated that you have skills in the majority of these areas, you may want to consider a leadership position. Some of these skills may be inherent to your nature while others may have been learned. You may have demonstrated these in a former position, with your volunteer activities or with family members. To develop your motivation expertise further there are a number of activities besides attending training that can assist you. These include volunteering to lead a task force, reading a variety of business publications, and talking to people who hold similar positions. First-hand expertise is often better than any textbook reading.

Another role of a leader is team building. Team building covers a wide range of activities in a business context. Team building involves selecting a team or working with an existing group, building and developing the team, and inspiring them. The characteristics for a team leader are similar to those of a motivator and may include permitting team members to develop strong and collaborative relationships and understanding the effects of change on human behavior and diversity. Other skills include inspiring, motivating, listening, questioning, and persuading. If leading a team is an interest for you, be sure to include it in your planning activities. Monitor any teaming activities you have done by listing the team building descriptor and the accompanying activity. Use the "Directing Statement Sampler" to help you produce your own statements that demonstrate your skills and abilities as an effective team leader. Notice how these are measurable and powerful statements.

Directing Statement Sampler

1. As Team Leader of the Take Your Children to Work Day Committee, I directed the activities of 10 employees to design a one-day program for 100 staff children, ages 9-15.
2. I directed a team of six customer service representatives whose mission it was to design a Customer Service Survey. I asked each member to create a list of 10 customer focused questions using my example.

Scientific

Employment in medical, environmental, and other targeted fields will increase in the next decade. This is a good time to include your assessment for readiness in these fields.

Careers in the medical field are abundant and diverse. When we think of medicine we usually consider the usual options like veterinarians, doctors, nurses, drug development, pharmaceutical, research, and development. The medical field also refers to home and personal care aides, skin care specialists, athletic trainers, medical scientists. Recent cutting edge developments in the life sciences have opened the biomedical and biotechnology fields where bio-chemist and bio-physicist positions are expanding. Most all medical careers call for higher education, but some only require a high school diploma, on-the-job training, and certifications. The skills required for life sciences and bio-technology includes science, math, engineering, and technology. Most also call for analytical, research, technical writing, critical thinking, and organization skills. Healthcare is an advancing field. The list of opportunities includes careers in hospitals, doctor's offices, businesses, schools, clinical trials, insurance agencies, research, education, and patient advocacy. According to the Bureau of Labor Statistics, other medical fields expected to grow include public and private hospitals, residential care facilities, and individual and family services. Much of this growth will be driven by the aging population and longer life expectancies. Your research and study of government career projections can give you an idea of the types of skills, education, and background needed for careers in the medical field.

An environmental job, also known as a "green" job is a newer term used to describe careers that protect our environment, reduce energy, and minimize waste and pollution. In order to sustain the changing environmental needs of the nation including the activities and requirements for existing businesses, the government has identified careers in green economic sectors. These sectors include positions in transportation, construction, energy efficiency, trading, forestry, agriculture, waste management, consulting, environmental protection, and regulatory affairs. According to O*Net, the Government Resource Center, these careers have been designated as in demand and require skill development. Careers in the green collar, environmental field apply to many industries including agriculture, engineering, manufacturing, science, administration, law, and construction. Some examples of the professions in these types of jobs include architects, hydrologists, environmental engineers, scientists, lawyers, curators, electricians, conservation engineers, educators, environmental consultants, and sales staff. Since many environmental careers are focused on science and engineering an advanced degree or licensure may be required. Other positions in the field usually require specialized training. Depending on the exact job, skills may include communication, public speaking, writing, research and development, problem solving, team work, and strategic planning. In the years since "going green" has gained favor, many community colleges and universities offer courses of study in preparing for specialized green jobs. A visit to the college web site, your local library or bookstore can provide further clarification. Check the National and state government offices including The Department of Labor and Workforce Development websites for possible grants to prepare qualified workers for environmental careers.

Every few years the Bureau of Labor Statistics updates the Occupational Handbook with data on targeted trends in industry and employment. Targeted careers are named so due to factors affecting the economy, industries, and population of the country. The government studies the changing demographics of employment, economy, population, education, and the industrial structure of our country to project industry and occupational trends. Trends are reported as statistics supporting either growth or decline in various industries or careers. The recent Occupational Handbook projected targeted growth for several major occupational groups like professional and related services, construction and extraction, management, business and financial, office and administrative support, installation, maintenance and repair, sales, and transportation and moving. Other positions targeted for growth can be found on the

Occupational Outlook Handbook or by visiting other Web sites like CareerOneStop.com where you can assess your interest and readiness for careers in the targeted occupations. Your state Department of Labor and Workforce Development Web site may also provide information on targeted careers that are more relevant to your region and to your interests.

Administrative

Managerial, financial, and secretarial are among the types of administrative jobs you might seek. There are many, but these seem to account for the most common jobs in administration.

Today's managers need to understand the job, the people that work for them and the process for getting the job done. As a manager, you wear many hats in an organization. You can be found supervising a staff along with carrying out your own specific work activities. Some of the skills needed by a manager include, team building, project planning and project management, strategic thinking, problem solving, risk assessment, decision making, communication, and staff development. There are many benefits to being a manager including better pay, higher visibility, credibility, prestige, and increased opportunities for advancement. Some people feel more comfortable being a subject matter expert while others prefer a leadership or management role. It is a personal choice. However, you may want to discuss your desire, skills, and abilities with a mentor or someone whose opinion you value. You could also schedule several informational interviews with current managers to inquire about the management practices in various companies or industries. You may be a manager in your current job or held this role in a former job or as a committee or task force member. Many management skills, including delegation, planning, communication, and organization are transferable from your volunteer activities. Further information and training on management practices are available online or through instructor-led classes. If you are currently employed, discuss training possibilities with your manager. You may also want to research your local college, county enrichment classes, library, or bookstore for additional resources.

Careers in finance are projected to increase over the next decade. Industries like securities, commodities, financial investment, real estate, and banking are expected to grow partially due to financial needs of the "Baby Boomer" generation (those born between 1945 and 1963). A sampling of the positions found within the finance industry include mortgage bankers, title insurance, real estate appraising, lending, insurance, tax, auditing, credit, and underwriting. Some positions are within corporate offices, others with financial institutions, and others with smaller firms. The skills required for positions in finance vary according to the industry but most seem to require people skills, analytical and problem solving ability, interest in mathematics, creativity, organization, and initiative. Should you need to assess your suitability into a financial career, you could schedule an information interview with one or more of your network contacts familiar with the field. You may also consider meeting with personal financial contacts such as your banker, real estate professional, insurance agent, or investment planner. They are excellent sources of information about the work load, office environment, hours, certification, and the overall benefits of being in that field.

Secretarial jobs include administrative assistant, or personal assistant positions. These require a wide range of duties and skills including scheduling, oral and written communication, project management, event planning, record management, confidentiality, organization and planning, problem solving, and the ability to multi-task. As an administrator you should also be skilled in computer applications, data base management, and using various types of office equipment. Some administrators are responsible for the workload of one manager, whereas others are responsible for entire groups or departments. Since administrators work in a number of industries, they are also knowledgeable in the processes and procedures that are commonly practiced in their place of business. Many trade schools offer coursework in administrative practices. Some of the courseware includes typing, budgeting, using spreadsheets, presentations, and filing techniques. You might want to visit some temporary agencies that deal in these types of jobs. There you can get free training and testing. Once you are sent out on temporary assignments you will gain experience and get to know people inside the organization. Insiders have a greater opportunity to get hired full time. There are numerous professional organizations for administrative assistants like the International Association of Administrative Professionals (IAAP) where you can attain industry-recognized certification, attend meetings and conferences, network, and take on a leadership role. You may already have transferable job skills that will apply to a role as an administrative assistant. Some activities include meeting management, event organization, spreadsheet manipulation, or manual design and development. You may use a number of administrative skills now that are easily transferable to a secretary position. If work as an administrative profession appeals to you, your network contacts or peers may assist you with skill development or employment contacts. If you need to polish your skill set, the library usually offers computing skills or you could use the tutorials that came with your computer system. There are a number of valuable on-line or instructor led course offered in most communities.

2

NETWORKING

Leslie Smith of the National Association of Female Executives defines networking as the process of "planning and making contacts and sharing information for professional and personal gain." Your overall network can assist you in uncovering insider information; those job openings not yet known to the public. These positions can come about as a result of organizational changes, retirements, new department structure, added budget for temporary staff, new or expanding project work, shifts in staff, reorganizations, and other areas. Networking is considered a highly productive job search activity, because as high as 85% of all jobs are found through strategic personal contact. Networking is about building and sustaining relationships, gaining knowledge, and ultimately finding employment.

Building Relationships

Relationships are established in several areas of our lives. "Networking Contacts" provides a tool you can use to plan and track your networking effort in personal, social, and professional areas. Sketch out a list of the people you contacted in the recent past. Include their names in the "Source" column. Fill out the method of contact, the name of the business, the date, and results of the contact.

```
Networking Contacts

Source              Contact  Business  Date/Result

                    Personal
Relatives
Friends
Neighbors
                    Social
Communities
Groups
Acquaintances
                    Professional
Peers
Supervisors
Businesses
```

Expand this tool as needed. The sources listed in the model help remind you about the contacts in your personal, social, and professional networks.

Personal

Your personal networking contacts comprise your relatives, friends, and neighbors. By enlisting their help, you are also soliciting their extended networking contacts. You may not find a job directly through your personal contacts, but your contacts know people who may be in a position to hire.

Networking opportunities abound with relatives, so think of any upcoming birthdays, weddings, showers, holiday parties, or reunions as opportunities to network. Since you already have an informal relationship with your relatives, it may be easier to enlist their support. When

39

asked about how you have been, your response should include a networking statement. Respond, "Great! I'm going back to work and looking for a new job. Can you offer any advice in helping me get started?" In most cases, the conversation will focus on your experience and background or on what connections your relative has. In any networking situation it is important to be prepared to discuss your background, skills, and interests. To begin, prepare a list of your potential family contacts and include as much information as you can. Your list should include your career focus, past accomplishments, and strengths to reinforce your focus and enhance your preparation. Contact your family network by telephone, mail, or e-mail. "Sample Written Correspondence" can help get you get writing.

Sample Written Correspondence

Dear Sarah,

We missed you at the reunion last week. It was great to see everyone again and please know that the family was asking for you. As you may know, I am beginning a new job search. My background has been in writing and editing clinical trial publications for the XYZ Company. With your expertise in this area, I would appreciate any advice you may have or any contacts you may know in the industry. I'll give you a call next week to set up a time to talk if that works for you. Thanks in advance for your help. I look forward to talking with you.

Our friends encourage us and we do the same for them. Our friends are those people that we can trust and count upon. This is reason enough to include them on your networking list! Another important reason is that friends have spouses, children, relatives, other friends, or relationships that can become extended contacts for you. Recall the many parties, sporting events, or dinners that you have attended. Frequently, other people attend and we often strike up a conversation with them. We should look at these meeting as opportunities to pass along our networking information. Many of us were not brought up to speak about ourselves, so these events are perfect for reaching out for the support and advice we need. It helps to remember that people want to help and will do what they can if asked.

Some research indicates that most new jobs are found not through our direct contacts but from the contacts of our extended circle of friends, family, and other relationships. It makes sense then to make everyone aware of your situation and ask about any contacts or openings in the business. Add your friends to your networking contact list and leave space for secondary contacts, like their friends and family. As you are planning your job search, give your friends a call and ask for their support. You may find that it is easier to speak with them to practice your pitch. "Sample Telephone Conversation" provides an example of a telephone call to follow up on a networking conversation that you may have had during an earlier meeting or conversation.

Sample Telephone Conversation

Hello Susan, this is Catherine. We talked at Judi's New Years Eve Party. How are you? I wanted to reintroduce myself and thank you again for

---

mentioning that you had a contact in the pharmaceutical business that might be able to help me with my job search. I appreciate that you mentioned that you would call her to introduce me. When do you suggest I contact her?

Enlisting the support of your neighbors is another good networking option. Your neighbors will likely not be in a position to hire you directly, but they have many contacts to share with you. Neighborhood events such as barbeques, cookie exchanges, walking groups, or holiday gatherings are good starts, but don't wait for a special occasion to network. Call or contact your neighbors to let them know about your employment status and ask for their support, contacts, and advice. Using the same format as for family and friends, practice and be prepared with a networking statement. At the beginning of your conversation, ask whether they are aware of any openings or have any contacts in your particular industry. You should continue developing your networking list by adding the names of your neighbors and follow up with them for details or leads. A quick note to your neighbor to acknowledge your conversation is considerate and it enables you to move forward with contacting the referred individual. "Sample Reminder Correspondence" serves as a model. Personalize your note as needed.

Sample Reminder Correspondence

Dear Beth,

It was wonderful seeing you and your family at the neighborhood cookie exchange. Thank you for offering to forward my resume to John Majors at the ABC Company. I appreciate your help and advice and I look forward to speaking to John about publishing opportunities with ABC. Do you suggest I call him after the holidays? Thank you for the connection. Have a very happy holiday.

"Sample Contact Correspondence" should help you think of productive ways to introduce yourself to the contact.

Sample Contact Correspondence

Dear Mr. Majors,

My neighbor, HR Manager, Beth O'Malley has mentioned to you that I am looking for a position in writing clinical trial journal entries. I realize that there may be no positions open at ABC at this time, but I was hoping that I could meet with you to discuss some of the newer technologies that I might become involved in at some point at ABC. I look forward to hearing from you. My telephone number is . . . I appreciate your assistance.

Sincerely,   .

Social

Social networking moves toward gaining contacts in your communities, groups, and acquaintances. These areas are less personal, but potentially as productive.

Networking within your community is an area that is beyond your neighborhood. Your community is those organizations to which you belong due to your own unique circumstances like your gender, age, or interests. These communities might be based on your field in which you specialize. We often don't look at our community activities as beneficial networking sources. When creating your list of social contacts, consider all of the activities that you are involved in with your town, for instance. You may volunteer in the school system, a scouting troop, the local food pantry, your religious organization or maybe you serve with a local not-for-profit. All of these activities have enhanced your transferable skills and provide solid networking contacts. The more community involvement you have the larger your network becomes and the more skills you develop. Continue building your networking list of contacts. When networking with your community members, be prepared with an informal statement like the one in "Informal Statement."

Informal Statement

I am returning to the job market, specifically in editing publications within the pharmaceutical industry. Do you know anyone in that industry that I could contact for an informational interview?

If a more formal statement is needed consider the example in "Formal Statement." A formal statement uses a technique known as the "elevator speech," a 15 to 30 second pitch about you.

Formal Statement

I am returning to the job market where for 10 years

> I specialized in writing and editing communications in the global pharmaceutical industry. My work has been featured in the New York Medical Journal. If you know someone in the industry I'd greatly appreciate the contact.

Your groups may comprise alumni associations, special interest organizations, community service groups, military, or professional organizations. On a local level, many people are now networking with other unemployed individuals in Job Search Networks. The purpose of these valuable networks is to provide mutual support, job search tips, and networking advice. Meetings can be found through your local library, unemployment office, or through Internet sites using the keywords "job search networking." Professional groups are another source for networking. These organizations usually have bi-monthly or quarterly meetings and it is advantageous to pay the local membership fee to become a member. Professional groups are very useful in that the members have a specific industry or position in common. Most members are already employed and may be the perfect contacts to get your foot in the door. Memberships can introduce you to associates within their organizations. They also reinforce your character and performance, so list memberships on your resume. Meetings usually begin with introductions, an opportune time to use your elevator speech to introduce you and solicit support. If you are new to the group, it is important to be prepared with a thoroughly rehearsed and prepared introduction. Your networking contact list will grow with the addition of your group members. Your speech should be succinct, automatic, and reveal your professional personality. "Groups Speech" provides an example that you can modify to suit your needs.

Groups Speech

Hello, my name is Catherine Jones and I am delighted to be here today. I represent ten years of experience writing and editing clinical trial publications for XYZ Company. I am currently in the market for a new position and would appreciate any contacts or support in my job search.

When it comes to networking we often forget about our acquaintances, those people who we meet or see occasionally. "Acquaintance Checklist" includes a number of people in various positions or occupations who you might meet on occasion. Next to the title, list the contact person's name and make an effort to follow up with these contacts on occasion. This is called a "ping." Build this list as you meet new people. Otherwise, you are likely to forget these individuals when it comes time to network.

Acquaintance Checklist

1. Lawyer
2. Doctor
3. Dentist
4. Veterinarian
5. Medical or dental office staff
6. Drycleaner
7. Hairdresser
8. Store attendant
9. Restaurant server or manager
10. Service station attendant

11. Exercise partner
12. Post office employee

Strive to establish some sort of relationship with these contacts in order to feel comfortable striking up a conversation with them. They have many contacts from their businesses and they may be able to assist you by talking to their other clients about your job search. They may ask for your resume or contact information, so be sure to carry your business cards or forward your contact information right after the meeting. Make sure to add your acquaintances to your contact list. Have you ever started up a conversation with a stranger while standing in a store or while waiting for your car at the service center? Sometimes these idle conversations turn into networking opportunities.

Professional

Your professional networking contacts are among the peers, bosses, and businesses that you have had dealings during your years in the workplace. If you maintained a cordial, supportive, and trusting business relationship with this very important contact group, it can enhance your job search not only as networking contacts, but as future business references.

Your peers should be added to your networking worksheet. They can be grouped into two categories; those people you have worked with on a daily basis and the professional contacts from your specific industry or profession. Your work peers have similar skills and are familiar with various industry directions and contacts. They have developed relationships with relative business contacts and they may be able to help you grow your network. These individuals are familiar with your skills, knowledge, and competencies. When networking for you, they will be better able to "talk shop" in regard to your specific strengths and skills. Your peer networking group consists of the people who work in the same business, industry, or profession as you. You may have met them at a conference or business event. If you are looking to find a job in the same industry these people are important networking contacts. You may want to schedule a meeting or lunch with them to explain your situation and to ask for their advice or feedback. Again networking is not asking for a job, but for developing collaborative relationships. When meeting with a group, be prepared to discuss industry trends, technology, training methods or vendors, contacts, and advice. Networking is a two-way street. Look for and forward any business information that you think might benefit your networking contacts such as technology, new business direction, and the like. Sharing gives you a good reason to "ping" your contacts.

Maintaining a business relationship with a former boss is another networking plus since your boss has far reaching industry and personal contacts. This is another individual that knows your capabilities. It is for this very reason that we should never burn our bridges when we leave our former jobs. Your former boss not only has contacts in your current industry, but knows people in other facets of the business. Your manager also has a boss and your network can continue to grow through that connection. As with your entire network, when you ask your former boss to network, be exact. Specify the type of position in which you are interested, the industry you are trying to enter, and the competencies you possess for the position. Try setting up a telephone discussion to discuss networking strategy and feedback. By now, your networking worksheet has grown into a workable data bank and you can see why it is important to have such tool. Otherwise, it can be nearly impossible to track and use your contacts list effectively.

We come into contact with many people in the course of our careers. These business contacts may be temporary or long lasting. They may comprise the people in other departments, people you have met at company functions or meetings, temporary employees, outside vendors, and other business relationships. These people are potential networking sources and they too have a wide reaching networking base. Imagine the vendor or service provider that you may have worked with who brought a particular product into your company. This source has contacts with hundreds of people in many businesses. You may have attended an outside training program with similar professionals from different companies. There is usually a list of attendees that is shared for networking purposes. You can widen your network by e-mailing or calling names on the list and asking for their assistance in your job search venture. "Communication with Business Contacts" can help you formulate your re-introduction.

Communication with Business Contacts

Dear Matt,

We met at the convention at the Swan Hotel in February. You may be interested to know that my employing company has been purchased by ABC Industries and that my role with the company has been outsourced. I want to stay in the industry, so I am wondering if I could call you to set up some time to talk about possible industry contacts. Do you have next Wednesday at 1:30PM or Thursday at 2:00PM open for a brief telephone meeting?

Sincerely,

Your networking worksheet is now complete and it is time to put it to good use in your job search venture. Keep in mind its purpose and value as you use it.

Gaining Knowledge

Although networking is a valuable tool that helps you find the right people that are able to help you find a job, it has other values like gaining knowledge about such things as hidden markets, company profiles, and insider information.

Hidden Markets

An average 80% of jobs are found in hidden job markets. These are markets that are not advertised and are filled or created for people who have been referred by a company associate, a recruiter or a vendor. There are several tactics to gaining knowledge about the hidden job market and they all involve networking on a personal, social, or professional level.

On a personal level, charting and maintaining your networking connections and deciding what to say or write in your communication is a solid start, but only after you've determined what you would like your network contact to do to help you. It is less threatening to ask them to keep their ears and eyes open for any jobs that might suit you, but that is not specific enough. You need to answer several questions. Do you want the names and titles of contacts? Can you use your contact's name as a referral? Can your contact introduce you to someone? Does the company have an employee referral program? Many companies have hiring incentive programs for their employees and your personal contacts may be able to recruit you. Since the hiring process can be expensive and riddled with uncertainty, many companies turn to their staff for referrals. If the referred job candidate is hired, the company will provide a financial incentive to the employee. It is a win-win situation for the company, the referring employee, and the newly hired. Your personal contacts may also be aware of other hidden job market workforce opportunities like business openings or recent headcount additions at a place of business, new products or services that will lead to an addition in headcount. You should make it a practice to read the business sections of newspapers, trade journals, or magazines to learn about emerging companies or perhaps about a new direction a company may be taking. Job opportunities are everywhere and finding them is possible when you know someone who works at a target company. Make it a point to check into these opportunities regularly and they should pay off. "Don't judge each day by the harvest you reap, but by the seeds that you plant" (Robert Louis Stevenson).

Your social network can also help you learn about the hidden job markets and you should be prepared to investigate these as you did with your personal contacts. "Social media" sites on the Internet like LinkedIn, Facebook, and Twitter are excellent sources for networking with specific audiences. These forms of media are the latest method to connect with people, business sources, positions, and industries. LinkedIn is tool used mostly for professional networking where you post your business credentials, build a network of contacts, join professional/special interest groups, research companies, and find job offerings. Many recruiters use LinkedIn to search for suitable candidates. Facebook is a more informal social site, but it is still helpful in your job search. While your contacts are mostly your friends and co-workers, the site also offers networking groups. It is a valuable tool to let your friends and group members know about your job search activities. Twitter allows you to read and send short messages, known as "Tweets" to your contacts, similar to "pings." This application, while short allows you to update your contacts. Tweeting can be done via a phone application or on the computer, so it would be beneficial to add it to your job search tool kit. There are many industry-specific networking sites, job-focused sites, and general job search sites. Another source is your former high school or university. Many have alumni networking capabilities, with tools, tips, and networking capabilities. Classmates.com offers a limited free service, but it allows you to connect with former classmates, further expanding your network. Social networking is just as important as personal networking and should be used as a vital component of your search. When using social media be sure to safeguard any personal or confidential details.

Your professional network is probably your best source for gaining knowledge of positions in the hidden job market. This group is most likely to stay abreast of changes and trends in the business world. Changes may be due to reorganizations, mergers, promotions, buyouts, terminations, or growth opportunities. The people in your professional network may also be aware of future job openings due to research and development or new technology. A helpful yet reasonable tool to use with all of your networking contacts is the business card. Many online sites will produce them as will your local office supply store. Your computer will most likely have a business card template as part of its word processing software package. In designing your card, include your name, position, and contact information. Have a number of cards printed and hand them out to your contacts. Give extra cards to your professional contacts so that they can give them to their associates.

There are several steps to open the door to the hidden job market through your professional network. With your special interest groups you could attend all professional group meetings or lunches, offer to make a presentation at a meeting, lead a discussion group or subcommittee, write an article for the organization's newsletter or blog, update the organization's Web site, or mentor a newer associate. To keep your name and your job search in front of your former manager, peers, and business associates invite them to connect on your professional business networks. There are many ways to tap into the hidden job market through your professional contacts. Through your persistence, preparation, presentation, and graciousness you will be ahead of your competition.

Company Profile

Gaining knowledge includes gaining information to formulate a company profile, something useful when you produce a cover letter with your application as well as in an interview. There are many ways to gain knowledge about the company involving networking on a personal, social, or professional level.

As with the hidden job market, our personal network can assist us with research and information about a particular company. In addition to business content they can also offer insider information about the corporate culture and the working environment. They may also provide input on whether your values, interests, and skills are a good match for the organization. Simple observations about whether the organization is cutting edge or conservative, its products, services, and culture may figure into your decision. Since your personal network consists of your close family and friends, you may feel comfortable asking them for their objective opinions on your image and communication style. These essential elements add depth to the job search as they convey who you are and how you can make an immediate impact. Studies have shown that it takes approximately 30 seconds to develop an impression of someone. Your personal network can provide candid feedback and suggestions on the image you convey. Consider your business wardrobe, hair and make-up, your smile, and your handshake. Do these each make a good impression, one that matches the company's culture? How about your communication style? Remember that about 50% of our communication is transmitted through our non-verbal cues, about 40% is based on our tone, and only about 10% is based on our actual words. Eye contact, open or closed body language, and nervousness are perhaps your most important behaviors to match the company culture. Practice your elevator speech and have someone you trust review it for all three communications attributes. It is also helpful to have them review your networking e-mails for content, style, and grammar.

Like your personal contacts, members of your social network can provide you with critical company information. When attending any meetings or functions with them, keep them abreast of your career situation. It is also helpful to use the Internet for finding information about the target companies. Sites like Facebook and LinkedIn are possibilities. Once you have identified the industry and position you are interested in, type the company name into the search engine to pull up a wealth of company data including location, products and services, economic data, trading information, and key leaders. LinkedIn permits you to search for these individuals. If there is a "News" link, click that to learn of recent changes or new products or services that may mean an increase in staff. Your connections and group members may work for those organizations and an e-mail to them increases your chances of being one of the first to apply for a newly created job. To make the best of these social networking sites try following the tips in the "Social Networking Checklist."

Social Networking Checklist

1. Complete your profile. Don't just state your name, position, and previous employment. Include a listing of your responsibilities.
2. Include a professional looking picture.
3. Connect with colleagues, peers, friends, and business contacts. You will be seen by their network of contacts.
4. Join special interest groups to network with more people in your profession.
5. Ask and answer the questions posted by group members. The more people who read your responses, the more people will visit your profile.
6. Ask your colleagues to write a reference for you and write a reference for them.
7. Be polite and respectful with all of your networking sites. Never use crude language or post inappropriate pictures.
8. Learn how to block inappropriate posts.

Your professional contacts are a valuable source for gaining new company information. When you update them with your employment status, you might want to attach any information or events you think they might find useful. This can include articles, links, newsletters, upcoming speakers, conferences, or training. Not only are you giving them something, which is the premise of networking, but they will be reminded of you. Invite members of your professional network to accompany you to special interest seminars, dinners, trade shows, or conferences. These events will introduce you to even more contacts and are the perfect time to learn about different company profiles. Being prepared to speak or provide a self introduction is critical because these events may provide potential leads. Articulating your career direction along with your unique value is known as "personal branding." Like selling a product, personal branding is an essential means of establishing yourself as an expert in your field. Branding encompasses several areas including your personality, enthusiasm, skill set, and competencies. It distinguishes you as knowledgeable, confident, and qualified all essential traits companies are looking for. One method to create your personal brand is to become a "subject matter expert" (SME) and promote yourself as such. You can strengthen your SME appeal by researching your area of expertise for the newest jargon, technology, and trends. Write an article or blog for a professional organization. Provide comments or answer questions for professional Web sites. Volunteer to present your expertise at a professional meeting. Teach a class at a local community college. Your elevator speech is another personal branding tool. Before attending any networking event, perfect your speech to show how you can add value to an industry or organization. These steps will demonstrate your innovation and will open the door to more professional connections and company information.

Insider Information

Business news, either in the printed media or Internet can open your eyes to factual data, but having a network contact inside the organization adds value. There are many opportunities to gain insider information using your network on a personal, social, or professional level.

Every few weeks, "ping" the members of your personal network to let them know the status of your job search. Share your interview notes, networking contacts, or other information to keep them in the loop while thanking them for their continued support. Your personal contacts who have heard of any organizational changes will most likely pass this information along. Due to signing a confidentially agreement, there are certain topics that employees cannot communicate. Also, the Sarbanes Oxley Act of 2002, also known as the Public Company Accounting Reform and Investor Protection Act states regulations for financial and accounting disclosure and certain company information again should never be disclosed. Still, your personal contacts may assist with their knowledge of upcoming opportunities or any potential prospects from members of their own networks.

By keeping up to date with your social network, you greatly enhance any chances of finding inside information leads. Your social networking sites are updated with company, information and new groups daily. If you joined LinkedIn, Facebook, or Twitter keep your contacts appraised of your search by making a general comment in the Network or Status Update sections. You should also make it a habit to sort through the comments of your Group Members. Also look into the big job search sites such as Indeed.com, Monster Jobs, and LinkUp for company information. These sites provide job listings by the day and hour. You can also sign up to get daily e-mail updates based upon your career interests. You may want to expand your social networking by looking for women-specific sites. These may be based upon a hobby or interest or are more professional in nature. Your community or volunteer social contacts can also supply insider information so be sure to add them to your worksheet. "Women Centered Sites" provides a list you might try.

Women Centered Sites

http://www.womenwork.org
http://blackprofessionalwomen.com.
http://www.karisable.com/women.htm
http://www.theglasshammer.com/
http://www.thetransitionnetwork.org/
http://www.mommytracked.com/
http://www.momsrising.org/
http://www.dol.gov/wb/

Many of us have profited from local job search networking groups. As mentioned earlier, these groups have regularly scheduled meetings where the members learn job search techniques and are wonderful source for contacts in the job market. Many times, the job search networking group assigns a moderator who is responsible for communicating open jobs and meeting dates to the group by either e-mail, blog, Twitter, or Web site updates. The moderator also reaches out to the community for inside company information and relays this to the group members. If you haven't already, research the job search networking groups in your area through the library or on the Internet. If you have the ability, volunteer to assist the moderator with the electronic administration for group. This will become an added skill to add to your resume.

Before networking was a job search term, it was used by sales people to develop and maintain business relationships that would eventually bring in clients and increase profits. We might want to follow the lead of the sales associate when networking with our professional contacts. Traditional business networking techniques include handing out business cards, attending meetings, joining the local Chamber of Commerce, and generally seeking out business leads. These days, sales networking techniques have evolved and focus on adding value or benefit to the customer. It requires understanding an individual customer's business needs and determining how your product or service can solve that need. You can replicate some of the networking tactics currently used by sales people to include the list in "Networking Tactics."

Networking Tactics

1. Actively listening to your contact.
2. Maintaining a professional relationship.
3. Forwarding the contact any information that they can use to solve their problem.
4. Speaking about your expertise at industry specific meetings.
5. Writing articles in related newsletters/blogs.
6. Displaying excellent interpersonal skills.

These tactics can validate your relationship with your professional community and let them remember you as a value-added commodity. Once people view you as sincere, skillful, and knowledgeable, they will remember you and feel more confident to share insider company information with you.

Finding Employment

Current Career

Ultimately, it is our responsibility to update our skills set to reflect changes in the business, including, technology, processes, and new developments. Reading industry reports and journals and visiting industry-specific Web sites can help as will taking advantage of free, low cost or company sponsored training. Once you have identified the skills and competencies needed for a similar position, an advanced career or a new career, you can begin to create the steps needed to develop yourself and cast your net wider. The career that you are comfortable with may have changed as new technologies or methods replace current standards. If you have been out of the workplace for a while, it is important to learn what has changed. If you are currently working, you will need to examine what other like- minded professionals are doing in the industry and learn how you can improve your skills.

Your personal network may assist you by providing the information, contacts, or resources needed to update your skills. To uncover needs in your current position, it is helpful to ask yourself some questions and then design a plan of action steps. Answer the questions in "Action-Oriented Questions."

Action-Oriented Questions

1. What skills, knowledge or new technologies are needed in my current position?
2. What competencies are needed in my position?
3. Where can I find this information?
4. What courses, readings, or white papers are available to improve my skills?
5. Which of these can I review locally?
6. How can my personal network assist me?
7. How can my mentor assist me?
8. What companies are looking for these types of skill sets?
9. Who in my network has information, or

A similar exercise can be done with your social contacts, both your group and Internet connections. The Internet is a reliable source for finding innovative and current trends on the skills, technology, knowledge, and competencies needed for a position. Job search sites are good sources for reviewing the skills sets currently needed for your particular job. Choose several to review to match your skills and verify if they are current and applicable. If they are not, decide on any corrective actions. It is also helpful to explore professional sites for job descriptions and to query members for information and suggestions. If you need to update your skills, contact your local colleges or the library for course information. Since many of your social networking contacts and group members are in your field, they are an excellent source of guidance and feedback. Another important step is to read through any articles pertaining to your line of work to keep current in your career, and then create an action plan to eliminate any gaps. Your social network including your professional and industry specific groups often post job descriptions. After reviewing these and updating your skills, you may feel more confident interacting with the group members and making use of their networking abilities.

Your professional contacts, especially those in your profession or industry are valuable sources of the current skills needed to effectively perform a job and of job opportunities. These contacts, especially the vendors, clients or customers are especially important because of their knowledge of outside clients and industries. After researching the current skills and business challenges issues facing your industry, let your professional network know of your continued interest in staying with the profession. You can also ask them to appraise your skill set against those which are currently in demand in the marketplace or industry. People in general like to help and they also like to be looked upon as experts. A call or e-mail to set up an appointment to review your skills and abilities for employment in the current field may be all that is needed to further your job search. An example is provided in "Sample Communication."

Sample Communication

Dear Stephanie,

As an expert in administration skills and a member of the International Association of Professional Administrators (IAPA), I would like to meet with you to review my skill set and provide feedback on my marketability as an Administrative Assistant. As you know, I left the HIJ Company in March and since then I have been updating my skills and competencies while trying to find another job opportunity. Perhaps I can learn more about IAPA in our discussion and plan to attend a future meeting with you. I will call you next week to schedule lunch (my treat). I look forward to seeing you again.

Sincerely,

Not only will you receive information on your skills, but your professional network contact may be able to provide other industry contacts or referrals. Make sure that you follow your meeting up with a thank you note.

If you have decided that you would like to stay in your industry but at an advanced or higher level, you can increase your network by connecting with people in those types of positions. Advancing a career often requires developing a solid personal, social, and professional network.

Your personal networking contacts can assist with new names, assistance, or advice. Prior to any contact, you will need to assess your current skills against those needed in the advanced position. "Current and Desired Position Assessment" helps to chart it. This exercise helps you compare your current proficiencies against those needed at a higher level. The chart will also help you prepare for any informational interviews you may have to discuss these types of positions. An example is offered in "Current and Desired Position Assessment."

Current and Desired Position Assessment

Current Position:
Desired Position:

Current Skills	Desired Skills	Next Steps

Armed with an understanding of the direction that you would like to take, seek out those individuals in similar occupations to gather any data to help your better prepare, develop, and advance. An example of how you might launch a conversation is offered in "Sample Telephone Conversation."

Sample Telephone Conversation

Hello Barbara. This is Beth Smith, a friend of Jodi Wilson's. I am an account coordinator for the ABC Photography Studio. Jodi mentioned that you are an account manager for the hospital. I am calling because I am interested in learning about the skills needed to advance in the field, particularly focusing on customer service. Could we set up some time to meet, so that I can learn more about what I would need to do to increase my account management skills?

Our social contacts are a wonderful source of information concerning advancement in our current field. The members in our groups and clubs have a variety of interests and backgrounds and may be helpful in our understanding of the skills needed for advancing our careers. Based upon your social contact with these members, you may have found that they display successful competencies and would be a helpful source of advice as well as networking. If you feel comfortable approaching an individual, ask if they would be willing to provide feedback on your job search, particularly your skill set. You may find, based upon your compatibility and interests, that this person would be a good mentor or role model. Share your career direction and interests with these individuals and get their feedback on how they see you developing to the next level. "Sample Opening Statement" can help you construct your own statement.

Sample Opening Statement

Amanda, I've been a Kindergarten teacher for two years and I would like to become a reading specialist. I know I'll have to earn an advanced degree, but I was hoping to get some feedback from you about any other steps I need to take. I know that you are a respected reading specialist at ABC Elementary. Can we meet for coffee one day next week after school?

Your on-line contacts can also provide interesting suggestions. In your industry-specific groups, ask a question about the skills needed for a particular job or job level. Specialists in the industry-specific groups love to "talk shop" and can provide you with very informative information. Start by making a statement about your position, years of service and the advice you are seeking such as training, particular reading material or other social networking groups. Since you are familiar with your current position and its natural progression, your professional contacts are good sources for advice on the skills and attributes needed for advanced positions within the industry. It is a good idea to schedule a short meeting to share your skills, core competencies, transferable job skills, and achievements. Try using the items in "Sample Agenda" to help you develop a well prepared event.

Sample Agenda

1. Purpose of the meeting.
2. Current (or past) position and its required experience and competencies.
3. Advanced position and your understanding of the required duties and skill set.
4. Development suggestions.
5. Other contacts in the industry.
6. Action plan.
7. Appreciation for time and suggestions.

You may feel comfortable having this discussion with your former manager, who can be a reliable source to discuss development suggestions and opportunities based upon your past performance. These types of discussions with your professional contacts are helpful in that they can assist with your focus and maintain your connection to future contacts and positions. After discussions with your personal, social, and professional contacts about advancement in your current field, you can better strategize on a development plan. "Current and Desired Position Assessment" is a tool that can help.

Current and Desired Position Assessment

Current Position:
Desired Position:

Current Skills	Desired Skills	Next Steps

Training Suggestions:

Reading materials:

Internet Sources:

Hands-On Activities (speaking, writing, leading, and managing):

Additional Contacts:

New Career

If, after careful deliberation and reflection on your values, interests, skills, and aspirations, you have decided that you would like a new career, your network can provide guidance and support. Your connections can work with you to define the training, education and markets needed for your career change. They can also help with any contacts they may know in your area of interest. Once again you'll likely find that your personal, social, and professional network can help.

Your personal contacts may offer to connect you with someone they know in the industry. It would be beneficial to meet with this person to further define the job to evaluate your interest and qualifications. The purpose of this informational meeting, sometimes called an Information Interview, is to learn more about an industry or position to further clarify your career direction. It is not a job interview but should be treated with the same respect. Be prepared with a copy of your resume and your business cards. The types of questions that you might want to ask during an informational interview are suggested in "Sample Interview Questions."

Sample Interview Questions

1. What types of skills are needed for this job?
2. What is a normal day on the job like?
3. My background is _____. Is there a way that I can use my former skills in this new position?
4. What is the job market like for this position?
5. Are there any particular classes that you suggest I take?
6. Are there any particular industry-related journals, magazines or web sites that you suggest I read?
7. Are there any professional organizations that I should join?
8. Do you have any contacts that you suggest I contact to gather additional information?

Whereas these are just a sampling of the types of questions you can ask, be prepared to speak of your background and provide examples of how you handled various situations in the past.

In your social groups, both personal and on-line there are numerous people with varied interests and careers. If, for example, you are in the women's club and another member is a marketing manager, you may want to learn more about her job or other jobs in that industry. A suggestion is offered in "Sample Opening Statement" that helps you produce an opener.

Sample Opening Statement

> Judi, as you know I am in the middle of a career search. I've been assessing my interests and skills and I have found that marketing, especially print marketing really intrigues me. My background is currently in human resources, but I am considering making a career change. After our next committee meeting next week, can we grab a cup of coffee together? I'd like to talk to you about what I need to do to change my career focus.

Prior to your meeting, you will need to review the steps you took in the job search planning phase and evaluate the skills, knowledge, and behaviors necessary for the new position. The Occupational Handbook, published by the Bureau of Labor and Statistics is a good research tool. Many advisory boards and committees have subcommittees like communications, finance, decorating, and fund-raising. If your career interests lead you to one of those areas, it would be advantageous for you to volunteer for that particular committee. The committee members may become new network contacts in addition to having a background in that particular area. Your on-line social network can also assist you. Your group members or contacts are a good source of information. You may also want to research other professional sites in your area of interest or join a professional women's site. You can join these sites and ask for career guidance from the members.

Your professional network provides information concerning industry changes, events, or news and suggestions of talented people to contact for career guidance. Their advice and insight is vast. In regard to career change, your professional network may suggest various activities to further define your interest. Some of these can include volunteering in the field or a related area, working as an intern or apprentice, or shadowing someone in the industry. They may also suggest that you work with a mentor or a career coach. As we discussed earlier, a mentor is someone who will work with you to define your current situation, and short and long term goals which allow you to reach your potential. Mentor's do not charge a fee for their assistance. A career coach will also work with you to define your career interests and goals. Since many are professionally trained and are independent businesses, they will charge for their services. A career coach will also work with you to provide assistance when creating your resume, cover letters, and interviewing. You can find a coach through your professional contacts, groups, or other members of your network. You may want to verify the coach's professional certification to make sure that they are fully qualified. Some of the services offered from a career coach are listed in "Career Coach Services."

Career Coach Services

1. Assists client define career direction and goals.
2. Provides candid feedback on strengths and weaknesses.
3. Encourages and motivates.
4. Networks on your behalf.
5. Requires that you follow up on activities.
6. Offers developmental activities.
7. Provides direction in a number of industries.

Whether you choose to use a coach, mentor, or another member of your professional network, it helps to get a different perspective on your career goals and skills.

3

PRESENTING

Presenting you can be complicated and we tend to put off getting started on the process it entails. "The secret of getting ahead is getting started" (Mark Twain). In this chapter we will look at presenting you successfully in the resume, in cover letters, and when interviewing.

Resume

Your resume is an important reflection of you and is your selling tool. It is your one chance to reach out to the employer and say, "I am the one you want for the job." There are many types of information to include in your resume, several documentation styles, and a host of methods to transmit your resume.

Information

Prior to writing your resume, it may help to gather all of your information in chart form. Later, as you transfer the information to a resume template you can identify the areas you want to include and those you may wish to discard. Depending upon the type of job you are seeking you will either produce a professional resume or a curriculum vita (CV) if you are seeking work in education. Each of these is produced differently. In the professional resume your work history supersedes other information. In the CV your education history comes first. Here we will concentrate on the professional resume. First, provide your name and a means to contact you at the top of your resume, followed by a summary statement that tells the reader what you do, who you are, and where you are going. After completing your resume, go back and take another look at this "impact" statement. Does it convey what you can do for the target employer? After this, some people list their top six skills. These skills can be a combination of professional abilities and competencies. The remaining three major types of information to include in your resume are work history, accomplishments, and education.

List your work history for the past ten to fifteen years. Include the name of the organization where you worked, its location, your title(s), and the dates of your employment. You may use the title, "Consultant" for any non-paying work you may have done in a volunteer position. Check for samples of other terminology using the Internet. Keep this section brief, but include enough information to demonstrate how your background well matches the job you are seeking. Eliminate experiences that are not relative. Go back and look over your history and recall anything you did in the line of work that is related to the job at hand and add it.

Provide your accomplishments that relate to the job specifications. Accomplishments are what set you apart from other applicants. Since a perspective employer spends about 15 seconds scanning every resume, your resume needs to stand out or it will get discarded. There are three basic steps to preparing your accomplishments. First, identify the tasks associated with your former jobs or volunteer activities. It may help to refer to a past performance appraisal or look up a similar job on one of the job search sites to use as a baseline. Jot these tasks in the appropriate column on your chart. Remembering your tasks will remind you of your accomplishments. Next, use words that describe what you did. These activities should highlight accomplishments in regard to saving money, time, or other achievements. Compelling wording and action verbs will enhance your description. You can find many helpful sources for resume action words on the Internet. A good reference is Resume Dictionary. Some examples include design, produce, led, develop, implement, create, manage, budget. Finally, describe the quantifiable impact your actions had on the company or department. You may also have saved time, made a process easier, solved a specific business problem, attracted or saved customers, or opened a new office. Think about what you did and the impact it made on your former job. These are the types of impact phrases that an employer is looking for.

List your education and training. List the latest dates first or list the highest degree first. Your education is usually listed on your resume as Education/Training. This area refers to your college education and any training or certifications that you may have received. If you do not want to reveal your age quite yet, you do not need to include the year that you graduated. Instead, state the type of degree earned, your college or university, and its location. Also include any honors or awards you received. If you went to college but didn't graduate, you can include the institution name and the number of credits that you achieved toward a particular degree. If you attended special training and you are certified in a particular job-related area, then that should be listed in the Education/Training section of your resume. Include the technical trainings related to your career interest.

Types

The types of resumes you should be able to work with include those that are chronological, functional, and targeted. Whatever type of format you choose, it is important to know exactly what information is needed for the employer to make an informed decision.

Chronological resumes document work history in reverse chronological order, describing responsibilities from your most current position. Once described as the most popular resume, in today's job market it has pros and cons. One positive aspect of the chronological resume is that many hiring professionals like the easy to read format. It is also useful if you are staying in the same type of position, if you do not have career gaps, and if you have made positive career moves. This is not the type of resume to use if you have had a number of different positions or have little job experience. Use the "Chronological Resume Checklist" to help you develop this resume.

Chronological Resume Checklist

Contact Detail: Name, address, telephone number, and e-mail address.
Summary Statement: Summarize your qualifications.
Professional Skills: Six priority skills you identified earlier.
Employment History and Accomplishments: Names and locations of the companies you worked for along with your years of service and job title. Describe your position by highlighting your unique accomplishments, abilities, and responsibilities.
Education/Training: Education and any specialized training.
Professional Affiliations: Relative memberships.

A functional resume highlights your skills and accomplishments in the body of the document and lists of your employment history toward the end. Since the functional resume focuses on your skills rather than your work history, this format is helpful if you are a recent graduate with limited experience, there are gaps or absences during your career, you are switching careers, or you are reentering the job market after working in another field. Many use this format to highlight the skills that were developed while volunteering. Some research indicates that not all recruiters or hiring managers like functional resumes since they are not easy to follow. An easy way to prepare your Functional resume is to research skill sets by visiting job listings. Search for the type of position you are interested in and identify the skills and competencies needed for the position. Review your skills and accomplishments and organize them into about three skill categories.

Every resume should be targeted or customized to a particular job. It takes more time to craft a targeted resume because it states exactly how your skills and experience matches a particular job. If you feel that your skills and experience compliment an open position, then it is to your benefit to write a targeted resume. Review the skills listed in the open job description to identify key words that match your abilities. This wording is usually found in the skills, responsibilities, or education sections of the job posting. Once you have identified these key words or phrases, create your summary statement and match your professional skills to the job specs. The remainder of your resume can follow a chronological resume format. There are many examples of targeted resumes on the Internet.

Format

After identifying the type of resume format you prefer, you can investigate various resume options. Look for templates, media, and applications that seem to work best for you.

There are a number of resume templates available on the Internet. You can also find them at places like About.com, Monster.com, and at your college career development office. Your word processing software also provides several samples. Look for templates geared toward specific job types. Although templates are helpful try to create a resume that follows some standards that are acceptable like those in "Resume Design Tips."

Resume Design Tips

Font Style: Stay away from fancy font styles. The basic Arial or New Times Roman type of fonts are the most preferred. Also use black type face. Keep your paper color choice to white or cream.

Font Size: Your font size should be 10-12 point size. You can make your resume headings a larger size but not more than 14. Your name and contact information should also be in the larger font and bolded.

Margins: One inch margins are the preferred style.

Bullets: There are a number of bullet styles available and the most acceptable are closed circles.

Shading: Shading is appropriate only in heading areas, but it is best to not shading at all.

Spell and Grammar Check: Use your computer software to spell-check your resume and check for grammatical errors. Ask a friend review the resume for any needed finishing touches.

With resumes, media refers to the format that you choose for distribution. Although the electronic version is the common method of distribution, make paper copies of your resume to distribute to your networking contacts or at career fairs or functions. Most companies today require electronic resumes and if your resume is not formatted properly for transmission and scanning, it can be discarded. Other sites that require an electronic resume are networking sites such as LinkedIn, Indeed.com, Monster.com, your alumni site, industry-specific sites, and any other site of your choice. To format your resume for LinkedIn, cut and paste your original resume and place it into the appropriate sections on your LinkedIn page. If you created a summary statement and a professional skills category for your resume, these would align with your electronic profile. LinkedIn has an edit feature, so you can always modify your profile as your needs, skills, or experience changes. Format your resume for electronic submission to a job search site or a company by changing the format to plain text, ASCII, PDF, or another type of conversion. Before beginning, read the site directions to see if there is a formatting preference. Don't provide a URL link to your online resume. Most recruiters stay away from Web links to avoid computer viruses. Also, if you have a newer computer system, make sure your documents are compatible with Word 97-2003.

Complete employment applications properly and thoroughly. The information needed on most applications includes personal information, employment history, your summary of experiences, available start date, hours you are available to work, any arrest or convictions, and some references. If you are completing an application in person, bring several copies of your resume, blue or black ink pens, the names and contact information of your references, several forms of ID, and a calendar. Arrive at the place of business dressed for an interview to make a good first impression. When you complete the section requesting your experience, use industry specific words to explain your background. Write out the application in its entirety, rather than ask the reviewer to see your resume for details. Since an application is designed to get similar information from all candidates, make sure that you proofread it to make sure all sections are accurate. Most electronic applications ask the same types of questions, so keep a copy of your resume handy. Most companies, recruiters, and job search sites require that you complete a profile and much of the information requested is the same as that on your resume.

Cover Letters

A cover letter should accompany every resume. Many recruiters and hiring managers say that they will discard a resume that does not arrive with a cover letter. The cover letter is a selling tool designed to catch the eye of the hiring manager. Your letters should be short, direct, positive, and focused on inviting you in for an interview. This is an opportunity to reveal a bit about your personality. Cover letters can be considered from the perspective of purpose, content, and branding.

Purpose

Cover letters serve general, networking, and specific purposes. They are not just for accompanying job applications.

There are several general guidelines for creating a professional cover letter. "Cover Letter Design Tips" can help.

Cover Letter Design Tips

1. Error free including spelling, format, and grammar.
2. Written to a specific individual.
3. Business-focused.

---

4. Demonstrates your understanding of the company and its needs.
5. Aligns the company's needs with your skills and experience.
6. Specific to include a FIIFT (What's In It For Them?).
7. Targeted including keywords from the open position.
8. Highlight 2-3 accomplishments.
9. Short, no longer than one-half to one page.
10. Energetic yet professional.

Cover letters are generally three paragraphs in length. Paragraph one should explain who you are and how you learned of the position. If you have the name of a network connection, this should be added to this paragraph. The second paragraph explains how your skills and experience can benefit the employer. In three to five sentences, you need to specifically convey how your skill set and past achievements can help the hiring company. This is the WIIFT. It is a match of their needs and your accomplishments. In this paragraph you are also showing your knowledge of the company or business. The final paragraph states the next steps, whether you would like to call the company or have them contact you for an interview. It is important that your closing includes your name, phone number, and e-mail address.

Your networking cover letter will be sent to a specific person garnered from a networking contact. There are three types of networking cover letters, each with a particular purpose. One is to set up a meeting to learn about a specific position or industry (informational interview). Another is to schedule a meeting to interview for an open position and another is to meet to discuss your qualifications (for any hidden or future openings).

To prepare any of these networking cover letters, it is helpful to outline what you would like your letter to include. Begin with doing a bit of research to become familiar with the people and the products involved. Know the competencies required for the position. Various templates for the various types of networking cover letters can be found on the Internet. Personalizing them will make them original and fresh.

Similar to targeted resumes, all cover letters should be specific to each position. Hiring managers and recruiters all agree that "blast" letters show a lack of purpose and are generally discarded. You can, however, create a general template and tailor it to each position that interests you. Most cover letters are written to a specific person. They contain your reason for writing, the position you are applying for, and how you heard about it. They also contain a brief summary of what you have done that is applicable to the position, matching the tasks stated in the opening to your professional experience. Include a call for action and close with your contact information. Since hiring managers and recruiters have a limited window of time to review a lengthy cover letter, it is important to be convincing in as few words as possible. Your cover letter is a selling tool. It is to your benefit to do your homework before creating your cover letter.

Content

The content of your cover letters will frame an introduction, a qualifications statement, and the next steps or calls to action.

The introductory paragraph of the cover letter is your first selling point. It should contain several areas including, your networking contact (if applicable), where you saw the opening and a link between your knowledge of the organization and your skills or accomplishments. It should be dynamic, free of clichés and statements that are retired or overused. A recruiter or hiring manager spends seconds glancing through a cover letter, so it needs to be attention grabbing. For an informational inquiry you should not enclose a resume, rather your cover letter is your request to learn more about a company or the skills needed for a particular position. "Cover Letter Sampler" can help you construct your cover letter or inquiry.

Cover Letter Sampler

Your colleague, Caitlin Matthews suggested that my qualifications meet your current needs. For several years I have been following the creative ways in which you market and present your merchandise. As a sales manager for Blackburn and Associates, I have opened three new stores and I was recently awarded the Innovative Marketing Award for our Rayburn store opening. I would like to contribute my expertise for your Merchandising Associate opening. Can we talk further to see how your needs match my qualifications? Would you prefer a phone call or correspondence via e-mail?

The qualifications summary is a paragraph that is used to describe your experience. Many recruiters say that they skim this portion of the letter before anything else. Since cover letters are meant to "sell," summarize why you are the ideal candidate for the job. Your qualifications need to be succinct and relative to the open position, using industry specific wording. Relate your experience to the phrasing used in the job posting. This portion of the cover letter is where you explain why you are the perfect fit for the job by tying your experience to the skills required in the job. You should also detail one or two past accomplishments that will illustrate your fit into the organization. Much of this background information can be found by reviewing the company Web site. There are also numerous examples and templates to follow to help you create the qualifications summary of the cover letter. Although this portion of the cover letter highlights your skills as they relate to a position, it is not recommended that you repeat information that is already provided on your resume. The qualifications summary is meant to expound upon your marketable accomplishments.

The final portion of the resume relates to any next steps or actions. This is the briefest portion of the cover letter and its purpose is to summarize your statements and request an interview or appointment. Your final paragraph should be succinct and assertive and express a desire to further the discussion in person. Some important points to include in your closing or action steps include your resume, dates and times that you will contact the potential employer, a statement of qualifications, and a professional closing with your contact information. Tips are offered in "Sample Call for Action Paragraphs."

Sample Call for Action Paragraphs

1. I look forward to speaking with you in more detail about the open sales position at Chris' Boutique. I will call you within the next week to see if you need any additional information and to set up an appointment. Thank you for your time. I look forward to speaking with you.
2. I welcome the opportunity to speak with you in person so that we can further explore how my qualifications and achievements can meet the (job specific word) needs of

---

> (name of organization). I will contact you next Monday to make sure that you have all the information you need to evaluate my resume. Thank you for your time.
>
> 3. I would greatly appreciate the opportunity to talk with you about the competencies needed to succeed in higher education. I will contact your office next week to set up a brief meeting. Thank you for your time and interest.

Your closing paragraph should be a few sentences and state a positive call for action.

Branding

We spoke earlier of designing your personal brand. Marketing a product or service is similar to personal branding. Marketing has been defined as promoting a product or service in terms of customer needs and satisfaction. Most marketers design branding campaigns where they create a name and image of their product with a consistent advertising theme.

The same can be said with personal branding for a job search. Personal branding is defined as standing out from a similarly skilled pool of job searchers by offering a unique value-added service. It is focused on selling your unique brand; your skills, achievements and performance that would benefit a potential employer.

There are several steps to creating your personal brand. The tools that you will need include:
1. Business cards.

2. Targeted, branded resumes.
3. Portfolio of your successful projects, papers, design samples and other business related materials.
4. Specific, branded cover letters.
5. Professional on-line business presence.

Since personal branding is about unique, value added propositions, it is necessary to identify one or two of your exceptional characteristics. You can find those by returning to the Competencies Worksheet that you completed in Chapter 1. By focusing on your top two competencies or particular skills you have begun to create your personal brand. Your next step is to create a listing of your achievements within those defined areas. Are you an excellent problem solver? How? Why? Is research and analysis your brand? Why? What have you done to support that?

Since the cover letter is the first impression a recruiter or hiring manager has of you, it is vital in these days of job insecurity that you identify what makes you a specialist, expert or a leader in your field.

There are a number of ways to format your personal brand in a cover letter. You can summarize your unique skill set in a paragraph by explaining how your background and experience can fill the open needs identified by the company. Another method is to create a bulleted summary statement emphasizing your particular strengths and achievements.

Another helpful cover letter to advance your personal brand is the T-format cover letter. In the T-format, the first paragraph contains the Introduction; the job you are interested in, any networking information and a powerful statement tied into the organization's business needs. The second paragraph contains the "T". Rather than writing a Qualifications Summary, you can create a column that matches the job skills needed by the employer with your skills and experience. A T-format cover letter sample is offered to help you produce your own.

Company Needs	My Skills and Experience
Strong Scheduling	Managed calendars for two department managers.
Strong Computer Skills	Proficient in Word, Excel, PowerPoint and Access.
Timesheet/Vacation/ Attendance data entry	Managed the time sheet process for 86 non-management department members.
Organization and Prioritization	Organized presentations Presented new hire orientations. Created materials and reports for all off site and internal meetings.
5 Years Experience	8 years experience as an administrative assistant.

The T-Format chart can be placed directly into the body of the cover letter. Creating it is a good exercise even if you decide to prepare your cover letter in paragraph form or with bullets. Whatever style of cover letter you choose be sure to consider personal branding as a means to set you apart from the hundreds of resumes and cover letters that will be received by the company or recruiter.

Your cover letter should be succinct and error free and contain the specific contact information for both the sender and the receiver. The information should be similar to the following salutation. It is helpful to have a contact name. Your social networking sites may have that information and it is to your benefit to research that before structuring your letter.

Barbara Higgins
136 Maple Street
My Town, New Jersey 00001
YourProfessionalemail.com

February 14, 20___

Mr. Michael Jackson
Accounting Director
ABC Company
123 Main Street
Any Town, NJ, 00002

Dear Mr. Jackson;

The body of the cover letter will vary based upon the position you are applying for and the style you choose. In the previous sections introductory, qualifications, and closing statements were presented. After completing the salutation information, your targeted or branded cover letter sample can read:

Your advertisement in the Daily Record for an Accounting Manager matches much of my financial and managerial experience. My background indicates experience and successful implementation in a number of innovative processes and controls. I have:

•Designed, implemented and maintained the annual fringe percentage analysis system for Our Company, Inc.

• Created and trained staff on General Ledger Account templates.

• Communicated with company leadership to provide leading accounting practices to enhance planning and controlling business objectives.

• Led a staff of five associates in budgeting and operations analysis

There are other areas of my background including my educational background, solid knowledge of Sarbanes Oxley, remediation and compliance issues that may also be of interest to you. I look forward to meeting with you personally to discuss how I might fit into your organization. I will call you early next week to schedule a time to meet.

Sincerely,

Barbara Higgins
908 555-1213
YourProfessionalemail.com

The Internet has a number of cover letter types and formats. If you choose to use these, make sure that you modify them to reflect your achievements and expertise and to add your own personal brand.

Interview

An interview for employment can be an intimidating process if you are not prepared and confident. Your confidence will come with practice, an understanding of the job and organization, and how your skills and accomplishments can align with the open position.

Format

Interviews now come in a variety of formats including networking, telephone and face-to-face meetings. Regardless of the type of interview you have scheduled, preparation is one of your keys to success. As you may recall, a networking interview has several purposes; to learn about a company or position, to apply for an open position, or to generally talk about your skills and accomplishments for a possible hidden position.

With any type of interview, you must be prepared to discuss your skills, accomplishments and background. In a networking interview you must also be aware of the company specifics including products, services and history. This type of interview should be no longer than one half hour. There are several suggested tactics for the meeting:

Do	Don't
Turn off cell phone	Be late
Ask if you can take notes	Talk about your problems
Establish rapport	Appear uninterested
Follow an agenda	Ask for a job
Carry a list or prepared questions	Talk about salaries
Describe your background	Present an unprofessional image with dress, language, or grammar
Listen	
Ask for suggestions	Offer your resume unless asked
Ask for referral	
Express your thanks in person and in writing	

A Networking interview for the purposes of learning about a company or position follows the same preparation steps. In addition, you should be prepared with questions such as:
1. How did you get into this business?
2. Who are the major competitors?
3. What is a typical day like?
4. What skills or education are needed for this job?
5. What are the types of entry-level positions in this field?
6. Do you have any suggestions for me?
7. What is a typical day like?

The goal of any interview is to secure a job therefore your preparation, questioning and ability to speak professionally and knowledgably are important. With a networking interview, your goal is to be remembered either for a future position or as someone that the interviewer feels confident referring to someone else.

The Telephone interview has traditionally been regarded as a pre-screening meeting to determine your suitability for an on-site interview. The meetings were quick and directed on your background, salary requirements and current role. Today, due to a number of factors including the large pool of similarly skilled applicants applying for a single position, the telephone interview is more focused, allowing the interviewer to differentiate you from hundreds of other suitable candidates.

A telephone interview should be treated as a face-to-face meeting and therefore you should be thoroughly prepared to discuss your skills, knowledge, accomplishments and knowledge of the company. To plan for the telephone meeting you should find a spot in your home to organize your job search material. It should contain:

1. Labeled folders of the open positions and companies that contain:
    a. Contact and networking information.
    b. Position and company details.
    c. Key words from the open job requirements.
    d. Your accomplishments in relation to key job descriptors.
    e. List of questions focused on these companies.
2. Pad of paper and pen.
3. Copy of your resume.
4. Calendar or computer.
5. A list of two or three strengths and weaknesses.

Other tips include:
1. Turn call-waiting off so your call isn't interrupted.
2. If the time isn't convenient, ask if you could talk at another time and suggest some alternatives.

3. Go to a quiet room.
4. Stand up (but don't pace). Standing projects your voice.
5. Don't smoke, eat or drink.
6. Smile.

Some typical screening questions can include:

- Tell me about yourself.
- What were your major responsibilities?
- What types of projects do you work on?
- What is your greatest accomplishment?
- Why do you want to leave your job (never bad-mouth your previous company)?
- Why do you want this job?
- What are you expecting in terms of salary (if you researched compensation for this type of position, be prepared to give a salary range if pressed).

Be specific and concise with your answers. It is important to listen, and watch your tone and modulation. You might find it helpful to prepare a list of typical interview questions and practice your responses with a friend or family member. The Internet has examples of typical questions and responses that you can tailor to your specific needs.

Receiving an invitation for a face–to-face interview or meeting is a significant achievement. Now is the time to polish your personal brand, review all company data, list specific questions about the position and company and be prepared to speak energetically about your strengths and accomplishments.

A company generally wants to learn three things about you:

1. Can you do the job?
2. Do you fit into the company culture?
3. Do you want this job?

Can you do this job?
Your responses to suggested job situations will reflect your ability to do the job. The interviewer will most likely suggest typical on-the-job situations, tasks, processes, or projects and ask you to clarify how you handled these situations. Practice your responses by reviewing the key words in the job description and tying them to your accomplishments. Be prepared with specific examples of your past behaviors and accomplishments.

Can you fit into the company culture?
Your knowledge of the company, major competitors, recent news articles, key executives and company values will show that you have done your homework and have an understanding of the company. Your responses and questions will help solidify your fit into the organization.

Do you want this job?
Your punctuality, attire, preparation, motivation and body language along with your knowledge of the company and your responses to the interviewer's questions will convey your desire to do the job. These qualities help translate your enthusiasm and eagerness to work for this organization. Some steps to follow to further prepare for the face-to-face interview meeting include:

- Practice your responses to basic interview questions.
- Review your resume and thoroughly familiarize yourself with your past accomplishments.
- Think of one or two job related weaknesses and how you handled them.
- Practice listening.
- Control your nervous mannerisms.

Most interviewers ask the same types of questions because they are interested in your ability to do the job, your motivation and your fit into their organization. The types of questions, the flow of the interview and sample questions will be provided in this section.

Behavioral interviewing involves asking a series of questions to determine your ability to handle various work-related situations. The interviewer is interested in learning how you handled a task or situation, rather than how you think you should handle it. Your familiarity of your past accomplishments, including the steps leading up to these, should be reviewed and practiced.

Most interviewers mix traditional questions with behavioral examples. Familiar questions include, "Tell me about yourself"; "What are you strengths? "What are your weaknesses?", "What make you want to work for our company?"

In behavioral interviewing, the hiring manager uses questioning techniques that are focused on the specific tasks and requirements described in the open position. The following behavioral interviewing steps will help you prepare for the interview.

Behavioral Interview Preparation

1. Review the job opening to identify the critical skills, tasks and job requirements. The wording is usually found in the opening paragraph or in the section entitled, "Job Requirements."

2. Review all of your work related and external accomplishments as they relate to these key words

and requirements. Align your proficiencies to the open position by identifying them by name, listing the actions you took to accomplish them and citing the results of your actions.

Try creating a chart to capture your past accomplishments.

Position: Human Resources Coordinator
Company: Gilly Stone, Inc.

Open Requirements/Skills/Tasks	Actions Taken	My Accomplishments
Design and deliver New Hire Orientation Program.	Reviewed current orientation. Researched reasons for attrition. Designed on-boarding plan.	Created New Hire Orientation for ABC Company. Conducted Monday morning orientation sessions for over 150 new employees. Attrition rate for new hires is 1%.
Excellent Organization Skills.	Prepare project plan for all tasks. Developed relationship with all staff by scheduling bi-weekly meetings.	Manage full HR project load to include recruiting, benefits, orientation, compensation and relocation for two departments and 250 staff.
4 years of Human Resources experience.		6 years of Human Resources experience.

Behavior interviewing is structured into what has been called the STAR acronym. When interviewing for information about past behavior, the hiring manager is interested in learning how you reacted to a specific task or situation. In addition, they want to learn of the steps you took, the results you achieved, and the problems and successes you had. This technique allows them to assess your skills, knowledge and experience using real world examples. The STAR acronym is designed to ask focused questions. The definitions below will help you prepare your responses.

STAR Acronym

ST- Situation or Task: Describe an actual situation or event from a job or activity. Do not generalize.

A-Action: Describe your role in the event. If the action involved other people be sure to acknowledge them but keep the focus on the actions you took.

R- Result: Describe the end result of the actions you took. Explain what was accomplished.

Some examples of behavioral interviewing using the STAR method of behavioral interviewing include:

"Please give me an example of a specific time when you had to work with a difficult customer. What was the situation? What were the steps you followed to correct the problem and what were the results?"

"In your resume you mentioned that you handled the relocation services for 150 college new hires. Take me through that process. What did it involve? What steps did you follow? What problems did you run into and how did you handle these?"

"You mentioned that you are proficient with creating presentations using Microsoft PowerPoint. Explain the types of presentations that you have created in your previous marketing campaigns. Who was your audience and how did you tailor your presentations to their needs?"

It is important to be prepared with STAR interviewing samples of both your positive and negatives situations. Take the time to prepare a STAR example of how you turned a negative situation into a successful or positive situation.

There are a number of behavioral interview and STAR questions available on the Internet or in various interviewing guides or resources. It is important to review the samples to get an idea of how they are structured and to choose several types that relate to the skills and competencies required for your targeted positions. Practice your responses to these anticipated questions. Some examples are listed below.

1. Describe the most challenging report or written piece you prepared. What aspects of this writing was challenging? Who was the audience? What was the outcome?
2. Describe a situation when you needed to cooperate with others to solve a problem. What steps did you follow? What were the results?
3. Tell me about a cross-functional team you led. How did you balance the various needs of the

members? Was the team successful in achieving the desired objectives?

4. Tell me about a unique approach you took to solving a problem. How did you come up with the approach? What other options did you consider?

5. Give me an example of an idea you had to improve your organization's processes or procedures. How did you develop this idea? What happened?

6. Give me an example of a project that demonstrates your expertise in… take me through the steps.

7. Give me an example of a complex technical assignment or project. What was your role? What was the outcome?

8. Tell me about a situation when you had to "stand up" for a decision you made even though it made you unpopular. What were the results? What was the impact?

9. Describe a time when you had to persuade a boss, superior or other authority figure. Take me through the steps you followed.

10. Describe an unpopular decision you had to make. Why was it unpopular? What did you base your decisions on? What was the result?

Conduct

The process for all interviews is basically the same from organization to organization. There is the greeting or introduction, followed by a discussion of your background, behavioral interviewing and the closing.

Introduction
Studies show that it takes an interviewer 30 seconds to initially decide on your fit. These critical seconds are based upon your professional dress, firm handshake, eye contact, smile and enthusiasm. The second part of the Introduction is when the interviewer explains the flow of the meeting.

Background
The interviewer will most likely begin this portion of the interview with a question such as "Tell me about yourself." This gives them an opportunity to listen and build upon anything you mention, clarify any gaps in your employment history and get a general feeling about what you have done in the past. When answering be succinct and focus on your past accomplishments and skills and not any personal information. You may want to relate:

- A career overview
- Your recent company and job title
- The role you played and its relation to the organization
- Your fit in the organization

You may also be asked about your strengths, weaknesses, long and short term goals, and why you want to leave your current position. This is a time to remember your elevator pitch and your personal brand.

Behavioral Interviewing
At this point the interviewer will begin asking you questions to ascertain your fit into the company, job and culture. As stated earlier, be prepared with STAR examples that focus on your skills, accomplishments and abilities and be able to relate these to the requirements in

the open position. You don't have to wait until the end of the interview to ask any questions. There may be opportunities to ask questions at any point in the conversation.

Closing
As the interview winds down the interviewer may ask if you have any questions concerning the company or position. You should be prepared with your questions about the position or company. This is not the time to ask about salary, vacation, benefits, or other inappropriate topics.

The flow of the interview varies with each individual, and interviewer. As the interview winds down, make sure you have addressed your skills and achievements and that you are confident with the next steps. Some things to consider for the closing portion of the interview include:

1. Your Questions: You should have several prepared questions. This shows the interviewer that you are interested in learning about the company and that you have taken the time to research. Sample questions can include:
   a. What are the short and long term goals of the company?
   b. What is the vision of the department?
   c. What is the company environment like?
   d. What concerns need to be addressed immediately?
   e. What do you see happening with this position for the next 3 to 6 months?
   f. What are the particular attributes needed to succeed in this job?
   g. What are the challenges a person coming to this job will face?

2. References: You should bring the names and contact information for three business references. Should you be asked for references, it is professional to distribute this information.
3. Next Steps: You can ask about the next steps in the interviewing process, such as the timing, any additional interviews or where they are in the hiring process.
4. Thank You. If you are interested in the position, let them know. Also thank them for their time and let them know that you look forward to hearing from them. .

Once you return to your home of office, it is helpful to write down any notes about the interview. It is also important to send the interviewer a hand-written thank you note as soon as possible.

All your planning, research, writing and interviewing are to be celebrated when you receive a job offer. Before deciding on the position, take some time to evaluate the job offer. It may be helpful to return to the Values and Interests inventories you completed earlier to help with your decision. Some areas to reflect upon may include:

- The compensation package including salary, bonus, 401K plan, stock options if applicable
- Company benefits
- Vacation time
- The work itself
- Title/position
- Training and development
- Start date
- Future career growth
- Company culture
- Proximity to your home

- Work and family policies
- Your manager
- Your peers

If you are concerned about compensation, you should be aware of the salary parameters of the job. This information can be found in the Occupational Handbook, from various salary calculators found on the Internet or from discussions you may have had with your mentor, career coach or members of a professional organization. Consider the following points prior to accepting a job offer.

Accepting an Offer:

1. Do not accept the initial offer. Express your thanks and gratitude for receiving it but make sure you understand the various parts of the job offer before accepting it.
2. Discuss the offer with family, mentor or close friends.
3. Negotiate if needed.
4. Respond in a timely manner.

After accepting a job offer it is important that you complete the company paperwork, including the offer letter in a timely manner. It is also professional and ethical to contact all the companies and people involved in your job search to let them know that you have found a job and to thank them for their support. Finally, maintain your networking ties with information, guidance updates and support.

"Own your change. Look back with gratitude but look ahead with confidence." Nancy Anderson

LaVergne, TN USA
07 February 2011

215566LV00002B/11/P

9 780557 317073